# What Could I Have Been Thinking?

## A book of off the wall songs, poems and stories

# Introduction

What Could I Have Been Thinking?

A book of off the wall songs, poems, and stories of life, love,
and growing up with regrets...
Well, not a lot anyway.

And then there's the occurrences of thoughts that of their
own volition have passed through this undisciplined mind.

As I think someone once said; It's elementary my dear friend
or pretty darn near.

# Contents

# Attorneys at Law

Ipswich and McGonigal
Attorneys at law
Ipswich and McGonigal
That, about says it all
So, lay back on that gurney
We're your representative attorneys
Here to see it's done within the law!
We'll count how many stitches, contusions,
broken bones and all
Relax my good man
We're Ipswich and McGonigal
Attorneys at law

Just sign the dotted line
Check or credit card will do just fine
Already, don't you feel so much better?
Knowing that, by the letter
Here we'll be
Taking care of you
And incidentally, while you're on that gurney
It wouldn't hurt
A moan or two
Remember, insurance soon will pay
We'll all be on our way
Bimini, the Bahamas
Sipping drinks in our pajamas

So, let me hear another moan or two
Ipswich and McGonigal
A check or credit card will do!
Attorneys at law
Are representing and taking care of you

Ipswich and McGonigal
Ipswich and McGonigal
No one else could ever do
Sign the dotted line
We're taking care of you
So, please don't interrupt out journey
Lay your head down on that gurney
One and all
And we'll see you in Bermuda in the fall

Were Ipswich and McGonigal
Attorneys at law
See you in Bermuda in the fall
Bermuda in the fall
We're your attorneys at the law

# Lives We Lived, Our Yesterdays

We live so much in long, passed days
In the times we call our yesterdays
Like the day that love walked in
The precious day you came my way

All big sparkling eyes
A smile brighter than an ocean sunrise
Could I say then I should have known?
That was the moment my love life had begun

And with you I'd be sharing the light of the stars
And stars, the warmth of the sun
The feelings of a need of each other
In a love we thought was like no other
The beginning of so many yesterdays
So many setting suns
In our yesterdays!

How could we know
That time would move so fast
And the silly things we'd do and say
So suddenly would become a yesterday

Did we speak of a love the world would always remember?
Of a forever flame burning
That could never become a dying ember
My, how time moves so fast
Yet we'll always in our hearts
In our DNA remember,
Wondering, asking when did the April-May
Become November?

When did a vibrant love and life came to past
When yesterday's memories are all that last.

Memories of yesterdays
Of sparkling eyes, warmth, passion
And believing life forever has just begun
To learn too soon our lives are mostly yesterday
And we are like the morning mist
That disappears with the rising sun

Too soon, too soon we spend our yesterdays
And like the setting sun that will rise in the morning
Go beyond life's mournings to smile because
Loved ones live as close as a thought
Remembering the best of times, not the mourning's
The days when we were mine
So, smile in the remembrances,
Sweet thoughts to lift the haze
Linger on those days
The days when we were mine

# Brand New Jew

A rabbi woke me this morning
Seems I fell asleep in the Cohen's seat
He said it was time I was awake and, on my way,
As he gave me a blessing, something about, what a day!
Here's a great mashugana, God! What a mensch
Then he said, why don't you give me that Tullamore Dew
I think you missed the Catholic Church by a block or two
Said he was running late, but a man named elder
Was bringing me a bagel on a paper plate

Then Rabbi Goldstein said, hey! Wait!
Let's put down the dew, learn a little Hebrew!
Perhaps we'll make this ganef a brand-new Jew!
Now, I'm thinking wow!
I could learn that Hava Nagila song
Find that black eyed girl that started me along
Become the best mashugana there ever could be
A brand-new Jew? Fiddler on the roof, that'll be me
Already? So, that'll be me.
What a nebbish can't you just see?

Now that I've been blessed, I'll give them back their seat
I've a hankering for Pastrami, Russian dressing on rye
A pickle what a treat!
A brand-new Jew, who woulda knew?
Not for me, that Tullamore dew
Manecheuvets, now that's the thing to do
So, look at old Jimmy, he's a brand new Jew
A brand new Jew!

# English Was Not My Major

My old English teacher
Would need to find a brew
If he were to read my lyrics
About how I say "I'm so in love with you"

Nouns, verbs, prepositions,
Adjectives if only I could do
Diagramming like mathematics
Is whoa to me if not to you

Proper English do I need know
For lyrics to ring true?
There are thesauruses and dictionaries
For help with words I hardly knew

Maybe he's retired and this will blow
Won't be so hard and new
Maybe he'll take it as a joke
Personally, I'm betting he'll need a brew!
Oh yeah! He's going to need a brew

# I Don't Mind

In great excitement we awaited the old, great Guru
Ascending to his throne so that we may hear his utterances
Wisdom and truth, words we came so far to hear
He looked upon his audience and spoke
"I don't mind!"

I don't mind?
Words of wisdom across all time?
Was he asking who?
Who really cares of our opinions
When across the world
people find themselves living day to day

Do we think they worry of what we may think
When some live with a bucket or bowl for a kitchen sink
So many people from different lands
Dancing and singing to strange bands
Stooped backs, leathery hands, leaving us amazed
Strange names, different drums
Yet the music somewhat the same

"I don't mind!"
Can it mean?
Think as you will
Call your god by any name,
My love for you will remain the same

"I don't mind!"
And he left the stage
Leaving us amazed
To ponder a dictionary in a single phrase

Now some may have been left confused
Some disappointed
Some feeling used
Or did the breath of intellectual thought
Come to clarity from a sudden bemused?

Written for the Ullmann's

# Doctor Help Me Cure My Blues

I've been walking barefoot through my life
In ripped up, patched up jeans
Can't say I've ever been exactly on the fashion scene
And I just finished a dinner
Cornbread, fatback, and greens

So, this story's 'bout my baby
You see she done gone and left this town
And I'm off to see the doctor
To tell him
I got me a bad case of the blues
And the doctor knows:
Leavings happen and never make the news

Told him my big-eyed girl headed north of Memphis
Hopped the midnight train
and I know right well
It's that big city called Chicago that's to blame

Now doctor, my physician
I got no girl to call my own
And I'm in need for a magic love potion
To salve my heart

Maybe in a month or two she'll call me on the telephone
Come on Doctor,
In your scrubs and soft sole shoes
You've heard me play this harp,
My guitar, zydeco, rock n' roll
But I can't chase these blues

And now I know what Muddy meant
'bout noth'en left to lose
So, my man, my Doctor!
A little something
Something to chase the blues
Anything to chase the blues

# Of The Manor Born

Used to dress in hounds tooth check
I was of the manor born
Prunes served with a silver spoon
Dutch masters hanging in my room
And a picture of a cow
Jumping over the moon

My butler Sammy shines my shoes
Shares his pot and excellent booze
He'd drive me around in the Cadillac car
Me sitting in back reading the rich man news
A half-drunk kid
In hounds tooth check n', shiny, shiny shoes

Now the Mansion's long gone, along with the spoon
Even the picture of the man on the moon
The thrift store doesn't carry hounds tooth check
And the Cadillac is one hell of a wreck
So, it's the bike or bus,
No need to make a fuss

The manor's now a fading dream
The blazer turned into a hoody and jeans
But I've learned that life's all about happiness
And my Dairy Queen spoon works as good as the rest
Glad I got that off my chest

Just see me my man, having fun
Hey!
Here comes the bus,
Got a run!

# Me and Jesus Having Fun

I just had to tell the man! Now!
I gave you cases of water
And you made it into wine
I said, "are you crazy?", that was Perrier, and
It was just fine!

He said, hey!
It's just one of my parlor tricks
I said Yes, I know! but please,
No more Guinness for the Mick's

He laughed and said
They sure love their brew
I remember the day
I made them Tullamore Dew
I surely do, remember the day, remember the brew

Then I asked, was that when,
They become the Fighting Irish
Just about then?
He said, "tell me about it!"
Laughed and said, "Ah-men!"
Well that's my buddy Jesus
A friendly, fun loving, happy Hebrew
I tried to get him in a Chevrolet
But he said nah! Love that donkey from the zoo

So, I meet his buddy Lazarus, he's a joker too
He thinks it's funny to nap in sepulchers
Especially when he knows
Jesus is coming through
Yep! With these guys, for a laugh, any parlor trick will do

Now we're off to the discotheque
The one they call the Well
That's where Mary Magdalene's always cast her spell
Getting stoned on some great grass
She always has enough to sell
And enough to knock you on your... anyway!

Then we're off again
This time to the Temple
Jesus said, hey! Let's have some fun
Let's get those money changers
Knock over their tables, take off on the run

I'm telling you, you've got to love that boy
He's such a bunch of fun
My man Jesus! Calls me the goy that knows when to run
Told me listen close my friend
It's not about guilt, it's all about love and having fun!
Got to talk him into a car, donkeys smell, and
OOPS! Gotta run! What crime did we do this time?

Hey, that loaves and fish gig sounds like fun
Feed the hungry people and then back on the run
Me and Jesus laughing and running, he is such great fun
I'm catching up but man that Jew boy sure can run
So, laugh and run with Jesus, find a life of fun
Laugh and run with Jesus, he's the man who invented fun

# My Bike Slowed Down Again

My bike slowed down, really slowed down
These pedals once so fast, barely go 'round
It's hard to keep up, hard as I try
And the only thing I know
Is the screaming in my thighs

My bike slowed down, so I'm thinking my way around
More air in my tires, new helmet, new shoes?
Cause even the smallest hill
Is giving me the blues
A skin suit? No more television news

This isn't my fault
I've done nothing but sit on the couch
Exercising my jaws, twenty pounds of new muscle
Then my bike slowed down
And people insist on riding and talking
When I can't even breathe
And the bike and me are in a tussle

My bike slowed down, really slowed down
Gotta stop by the bike shop see what it can be
A little lubrication, maybe they'll ... lie for me?
New peddles? No way can it be me
Twenty new pounds, every hill a frown
Wow! My pants belt still goes around


If only I could ride hills, that only go down
What's the matter with this bike,
Why in the world did it slow down?
Off to the bike works in old Doylestown
Hope they don't answer my questions with a frown

# Ain't No Mondays No More

Ain't no Mondays no more
My mind just retired today
I'm the only one listening
To what I have to say
But here's the good news
Threw out my work shoes
Gonna sleep as late as I choose
Drink coffee, read the news
I might throw out the V-8
Bloody Mary's after eight
If I choose
Did I say, I threw out my old work shoes?

Cause there ain't no Mondays no more
The dog and me
Practicing our snore
I'll say look the sun's up,
You feel like getting up pup?
Or should we just lie here some more?
No more ticking time clock
No more driving in the morning dark
No more boss, no quotas
Or paperwork to be tossed
I just heard myself say
"might ride my bike today"

Oh yeah! I just retired today
Gonna fill my life with play
I might watch the Mayan's mow the lawn
Ask them what they were thinking
Their calendar making's really stinking
Or was it our anthropologist
Who got it all wrong?
Hey, but what do I care!
Think I'll just go on singing my song
Or maybe write a new score
One about ain't no Mondays no more

Man! That puppy can snore!
Singing "ain't no Mondays no more"
Ain't no Mondays no more

# Fatstockie in Limerick

Ah! Yes, it's Prince Fatstockie
From the Saudi country to Limerick
And the town of Athae, crying Allah-Akbar
It's all he could say
And do you know, he can't figure out
That guy from Nazareth to this very day

Now he shared a local libation called Guinness
And after four of five flagons
It's been said, he couldn't tell his end from his beginest
Then from the Mediterranean he called his yacht
Saying, give me a few good Irishmen
Some that can some that cannot

At Brown Joe's he shouted, Allah-akbar
As the lads in the pub said, fill the glasses again
Or we're not going very far
Now fat ass Fatstockie in his flowing robes
Couldn't step dance to save his very soul
So! Up steps Kelly the Brian, singing the "Patriots Game"

Yes, to tears in their beers
It's always the same
Now you know how Jesus became a Spanish name
So, what were we talking about?

Oh yeah! Brian Kelly and the Patriot game
A pint of Guinness, the lads singing
In no particular refrain

# Flying to New Orleans

I'm flying to New Orleans
To walk up and down on Bourbon Street
Gonna do some crawfish, get some oysters shucked for me
Flying to New Orleans, wondering what else I'm gonna do
When an angel sits down next to me
We share how do you do's
Now my luck's just gotten better
Let me tell you, so has the view

She's a long-legged beauty, red curls in her hair
Asking where I'm going, what I'm gonna do down there
Then she asked where I'm staying, am I lookin' for some fun
Now my heart is saying yes to me, my mind is saying run

I'm flying to New Orleans, wasn't looking for someone
But now she's calling me sweetie
Said let's go and have some fun
Said to forget my shyness, cause there ain't no place to run
Now she could be an angel,
You know we're flying pretty high
But ain't no way an angel,
could have that mischief in her eye

I'm flying to New Orleans, wasn't looking for someone
But you know the lady sitting next to me,
Well she could be the one!
I just called her lover,
said that's the best offer I've had today
how 'bout's we go have some fun
then told her not to worry, I don't know how to run!
And if I took to running tell you where it'd be

Anywhere this angel said that she would be with me


We'll be together in New Orleans, down on Bourbon Street
Sharing Cajun love and music, maybe even stop to eat!
And let me tell you brother I won't go flying anywhere
Unless it's with this angel sitting next to me,
With the red curls in her hair
Yeah! We're flying to N'Orleans
Flying to N'Orleans
Yeah, I'm flying to N'Orleans with this long-legged angel
With the red curls in her hair

I'm flying to New Orleans
To walk up and down on Bourbon Street
Gonna do some crawfish, have some oysters shucked for me
Flying to New Orleans wondering what else I'm gonna do
When an angel sits down next to me
We share how do you do's
Looks like my lucks just gotten better
Let me tell you so's the view
I've just forgotten Bourbon Street
Or where this plane is going to

I'm flying to New Orleans
Let's get this plane down on the ground
We're wasting time now flyman
Get us down to N'Orleans town
Come on Mister Pilot get us down to Bourbon Street
It's getting to the point that I can't stay in my seat


24

# The Aromatic Man

Aqua makes his bones so supple
If only the boys in the band,
Knew it was the water of love
Add a little Velva and Pop-Pop
Smells better than those
Swift, handsome, singing angels from above

He only needs to stand in the streets
And the ice cream truck will stop
And bring him free treats
In the coffee shop needless to say,
The waitress will bring lattés all through the day
And the wink in her eye says Pop-Pop you're more than ok!

Women brush up against him
Hoping the scent will rub off
Such pride he takes in being the Aqua Velva man
Not his friend on the axe...Boris Karloff
He always knew jealousy would follow
That his popularity would be hard to swallow

He always said "I wish the band could smell as well"
But then again, guess I'm not just another fish in the sea
I just smell so swell, yet again, that's just me
Yeah, yeah, yeah
The Aqua Velva Man, who else could it be?
Pop-Pop maybe,
A small squirt for me?

# A Ball of Fluff and Shih Tzu Eyes

I had him now, a ball of fluff
With the most expressive Shih Tzu eyes
He slept on my lap all the way home
We were on our way to be pals
Constant companions for seventeen years
Seventeen years he spent training me,
On how he thought life should be

The funniest, smartest, prettiest boy
Children thought of him as a furry toy
Neighbors actually knocked on the door,
Asking could they take him on a walk
And sit with him for a while
What a true blessing across the years
And although he has been gone over two years,
Just these thoughts bring me to tears

Was he my shadow or was I his?
Wherever we traveled, wherever we went,
Better time was never spent
When he got something in his head,
He'd never relent
He once took time to teach a full-grown Timber Wolf,
Who was actually the alpha
The wolf never could figure him out, thank god!

Buster, Bussy, baby boy
My granddaughter always asked,
Why didn't I name him Fluffy?
If you passed him on the street and didn't make a fuss,
He would turn around puzzled, "didn't they see me?"
If you welcomed him into your house,
Right to the kitchen, bark at the sink
"where is my water?"

It was very rare for him to take a treat and eat it immediately
He would hide it in plain sight (we called it his inventory)
When he was ready, he would go bark at it,
Then he would eat it!
So many crazy things he'd do
A family of ducks would line up behind him,
And follow him around
The local heard of deer thought he belonged,
as he walked amongst them
I think they liked his big, white, fluffy tail

Oh yes!
If you came to his house, you could not stand and talk
You had to sit down, no standing and talking
What a crazy guy, what a personality
What a hole in my heart

# Pretty Girls [Can Do Anything]

Tattoos, ugly shoes
Big eyeglasses, hair of blue
A pretty girl can get away with almost anything,
Anything that she may choose

Five earrings, ripped up jeans
A pout and smile, and I'm a yo-yo on her string
Pretty girl, pretty girl
Gets away with almost anything
Anything!

Tattoos, blue jeans
Baby you know you're gonna be
My every day, real life dream
Rings on your fingers
Rings on your toes
Kiss that diamond on the side of your nose

Azure blue hair, soon to be pink
Bright red lips, nothing else can I think
But to kiss those lips, hold you so near
Say, be who you are,
But while you're getting away with everything
Take me with you my dear

Whatever you want to do,
Baby I'm with you!

# Broken Hearts are Free

Hey love, don't want to hear
About your old friend
We don't even care
If he was "William the Penn"

Let it go, for can't you see
Everyone, everyone's been hurt
Oh yeah! Broken hearts are free in this here galaxy
No one escapes,
Not you, not me

So, don't be a martyr
Cause those guys are all dead
Go find someone that you can laugh with
And share a bed

Come to think of it
If he was, William Penn
I don't think I'd want him for a friend, not me
Just can't see it
Me drinking beer, him drinking tea

Time to move on with life
Even if psychologists were cheap or free
In the end they're going to leave you adrift
All by yourself, on the deep blue sea

So find someone fun, tell them the sex is free
Say I'll know, if and when you're in love with me
If not! Nothing lost, we had fun and the love was free!

# Cross Country, Val, and Buster

Dear Valery,
I need your help, maybe you can explain cross country to Buster
He was very puzzled upon leaving Lehigh University
And the Paul Short invitational
These are the questions I endeavored to answer
However, I have not been able to get the idea across to him

He was stunned that so many people,
Men and women
Came out in their underwear on such a lousy day
"Didn't they realize how muddy it was?"
"was that why the underwear,
They didn't want to get their clothes dirty?"

Every so often a whole bunch of them, surprisingly
The men all went chasing off together,
Then the girls did the same thing

Now there they went, more people than I ever saw
Walking down the street, chasing something down that field
I never did see just what they were chasing

Then someone shouted, "Let's go to the mile mark!"
And another big group
(these people were all wearing clothes, mixed men and women)
Ran up a hill

Well what do you know?
Here come all the girls in their underwear!
Spread out in a long line, and there again,
Whatever they were chasing must have had a big lead
Buster figured it must be a cat
Nothing else could make that many people that mad
Had to be a cat!

All of a sudden here come the boys in their underwear well,
By this time, even the people in their clothes were mad at that cat
Because they were all screaming "Go get him!"
"Come on Bill!" "Come on Tom!" "Go get him!"

So, guess what?
There was even a Saint running in his BVD's, no kidding!
A lady beside me yelled come on Saint Joe!
Anyway, I've got to think these have to be the dimmest people
I've ever seen in one group
Or could you explain to me why not even one of them figured out
Hey! Why don't I wait right here
And see if that damn cat doesn't run home!

Because apparently, that is exactly what happened, yes,
Lo and behold Jim (Chief) takes me right back,
To where everyone started chasing
And here they come! Spread out over God's half acre
Mud all over themselves and their underwear

All the people in their clothes are still screaming
Get her! Pass her! Way to go Val! Way to go Danny!
But once again I still didn't see
What in the world they were after

And I think at this point they were all so tired and dirty,
That they didn't care that it got away
Another thing that puzzled me is that
After the first group couldn't catch it,
Here comes another group running in the same direction?

All I can figure out is it has something to do with
Putting people out in the rain in their underwear,
If you shoot a gun at them,
They will all start running away from the noise
And chase something, anything, I never did see it!
Chief said maybe they'll get a medal, makes no sense to me
What are you going to do with metal? Throw it at the cat?
I mean a Saint wouldn't do that! Would he?
Boy cats can make anybody mad!

Thank You!
Buster the Shih Tzu

P.S. saw you chasing, maybe you can help me
make some sense out of all this (the Chief is useless!)
I'm sorry but I never did see what that rascal looked like!
Oh yeah! It really was great seeing you!

34

# The Flim-Flan Flip Flop Man

Seems I've always admired the Jews
They seemed so smart to me
Until of course I got to thinking
About the greatest flim-flan man to this very day
So already? Let me tell you! He did it without blinking
But not to worry, there'll be no hell to pay
It's just a biblical story that unravels, this way

Seems Moses found the tribe,
And he said, come 'n follow me
I'll take you to the promise land, wherever that may be
So, he hopped on the horn to the factory
Ordered ten thousand flip-flops
Said pull out all the stops!
That should hold em 'til we get somewhere near the Galilee

So, Moshe, already!
The price by the time we get there,
Just you wait 'n see
So! You people in Ocean City
thinking flip-flops just came about
No, for forty years he kept them walking
Ah! So once in a while, a little squawking?
Lost for forty years, you kidding me?
Pretending he's lost, roaming across, the land of Galilee

Back and forth across the desert,
Selling shoes to the traveling Hebs
No, no credit cards, oh! No indeed
Not for Moses, the flim-flan man from Galilee

So, just keep that factory cranking
I'll keep them here long as can be
Come on you Jews, you'll need new shoes
Come on and follow me

Once heard him say, selling shoes
Under the "Promise Land" brand
Is gonna be the death of me
Wondering around with no GPS
in the land of the dried-up sea
Moses was the man, forget Nike!
The greatest salesman forever to me
Sorry but those old Jews had to be dumb,
Even dumber than can be
Yeah, one wrote down he saw a man get out of his boat,
Walk across the sea, give me a toke, let's see, "what I see"

He had them eating manna
While he was getting delivery
Ah! No thanks, no Gelfite fish or octopus for me
Now I gotta laugh, whenever I see flip-flops,
On the street or by the sea
Pardon, have to get the door, be right back
That delivery's for the man and me
The great flim-flan man, like! So, he couldn't find the sea?
Number one flim-flan flip-flop man from the land of Galilee

Now you know the rest, the rest of the story
Forty years of making a buck, finding fame in sales
And how about all that, biblical glory!
Bet you never knew shoes was the truth of the story

# Wait a Minute!

You know, you know
You are the girl of my dreams,
Anytime I am with you
Yet, when you go away
I get so lonely and so blue
Then those green eyed, blue eyed, brown eyed girls
Wait a minute!

You know I love you so, when I am with you.
Then! there's those lovely girls,
Well they tell me they can help me to get through,
Those dark, dark moments when I'm without you
Seems they can't stand
Me being so lonely and so blue
Wait a minute!

You know baby, you're the girl of my dreams
And I just get caught up
When those girls try their schemes
What's a guy to say?
When they start slipping
Out of their jeans?
Wait a minute!?

So you got to help me baby
Cause when we're together,
Those people don't come my way
So, please don't leave me alone for any moment of the day
Girl of my dreams, reason for my schemes
Let me love you every day

37

And wait a minute are words
One more minute
Another minute
One more minute with you
I won't have to say

# Harry the Jew (Salesman of the Year)

I went to the fish market for dinner
And there I met him, Mr. Harry the Jew
I went to buy some fresh fish
Walked out in his shoes
Said, he had no fish, but to look at me!
Standing there in shoes that, just won't do
Said, if he had a scissors, I'd have just the shirt for you

Said he had no fish, but for a buck
I've a bagel, some cream cheese too
It will fill you up, and those shoes
Will fit better in a day or two
Salesman of the year, August member of the tribe
Told, he sold a synagogue to the Rabbi
With a bike, no one could ride

Harry would say, hey Morey! Don't he look good?
Shoes make the man
How about a good price on this tie?
You know, it's the tie that makes the guy!
That's Harry, the man could sell an empty can of beans
Sell most anything
Fishman with chutzpah, saying "oh, sure, by all means!"

Harry the Jew, Harry the Jew
He's got no fish, but make you look at your shoes
A buck for a bagel, chutzpah but no beans
Best damn salesman I've ever seen

# The Lighting of the Tree

It's the lighting of the tree in the old town square
And for everyone's care they've shut down the town
Seems everyone's here
And in only minutes the big man himself will lead the cheers
Riding along in a fireman's chair
Up the street leads the high school band
Playing Santa's favorites of good will and good cheer

There is overwhelming anticipation and electricity in the air
Parents calling, look there he is, look Santa's here!
He moves while waving to the crowd up to the darkened tree
And the countdown begins
10, 9, 8, 7, 6, and Pow!
There it stands so beautiful, lit up so bold
They've been doing this for over a hundred years
I've been told

The crowd is dispersing, getting out of the cold
To their favorite restaurant to chase the chill and shivers
Laughing, smiles all around
Now it's official the season is here
Children's energy levels off the scale
And not about to slow down
After all Santa's in town!
We saw him light the tree to cheers and applause
Yes! We saw it ourselves
Santa's in town, Santa's in town!
Smiles and greetings all around

# Too Much Thanksgiving [Can There Be?]

I really should walk the dog
Or in the fireplace put another log
But turkey lethargy's come over me and my eye lids
Keep falling until I can't see
Oh yes! I know there should never be
Seconds for me!
I'm now overstuffed as a turkey can be
Ah! Is that pumpkin pie and whipped cream that I see?

We've finished the turkey
That "Thanksgiving turkey"
That announces the beginning of the holidays
Didn't really need that pie, I was already well fortified
So, in my favorite chair, I sat down with a sigh
There's a game on the telly
But after all the dressings, mashed potatoes
I've seen better days, the worlds becoming a sleepy haze

So instead of running a lap, think I'll take a nap
Apple pie did you say? My goodness what a day!
Too much Thanksgiving, can there be?
I think my stomach might agree
Yet of course, you never want to insult the cook
I just don't have that in me
Coffee or tea?
Cookies?
Well let's see
Turkey sandwich?
Okay I'm getting up!
Maybe half a cup

# Some Kind of Friend

Some kind of friend you turned out to be
Worse than a leaky boat in the middle of the sea
Speak of bailing out? It is my money running out
You went and spent all the money
And that's no joke, not even kind of funny!
Some kind 'a friend you turned out to be

Saw you in that Cadillac, said holy cow!
Holy cow what have you done now?
And doesn't along come officer Slavin saying
Come on and follow me!
Me, I'm saying there's no money left for bail
Now what's going to be? As Officer Slavin's telling me
I could leave him there just down the street in the jail
And for a dollar eighty-three, he'd even throw away the key!
He got me thinking, friend this is the end
Totally out of bail, sure hope you like that jail
Yep, Officer Slavin, wasn't me
After all,
Jimmy McKernan's probably where he was meant to be.

You know this could work well for me
McKernan saying, what kind of friend you turned out to be!
Yeah, it will be a while before he'll share a toke with me
But the money's spent, we lost the key
Hey three hots, a cot, clean clothes
No reason to go on searching for the key
Some kind of friend I turned out to be!

# Doctor Southern Comfort

Doctor told me this would work,
That I'd get over you.
First, we'll meet and greet down the street
At The Lucky Shoe
We'll say hello over a shot of Southern Comfort, or two?

Well sure enough, there she was
A couple bar stools away,
Speaking softly, making my day.
Eyes that said I like you too!
As she, the doctor and me shared a shot
Or was it three or two?

Doctor said, she'll help you chase those blues
But still, a little hurt remained
Until she flashed those baby blues
So! Here I am thinking, man!
What do you have to lose

So! I call him Doctor Southern Comfort,
Prescribing Bourbon to chase the blues
A little sweetness in your cup,
Beautiful new friends showing up,
Learning I've got nothing left to lose

A new baby, me, my physician Doctor booze!
He's my physician Doctor booze!

# A Full Confession

It was Officer Slavin asking me, what! Did I do wrong?
I asked, do you mind if I explain it in a song?
He said well that will be a first
But, then again, I'm sure that I've heard worst

So, I sang
Officer not quite father confessor, I have sinned!
Most of which,
probably for the moment I should keep with-in
besides if I told you,
I'd have to take the fifth
(Jamison or Tullamore Dew)
Try as I might to get away with it,
But stay with me you can't go wrong
There very might be another verse to this song

Another verse of a life gone wrong
But, knowing that Irish cops always love a song
Now, I never got caught, never used a gun
They couldn't catch me, not as long as this boy could run!
And as long as I'm confessing,
Inside this mind I've done a little messing
Truth be told,
There have been times I've been a little bold

So, Officer Slavin, don't you think it's time I went to bed
Let the Dew slowly settle in my head?
So, there it is, my confession
Please don't make me write out all my transgressions
Now! Would ya like a wee taste a Dew?
A nip, just a wee nip,
And we'll keep all this just between me 'n you.

# The Tribe that Loves Snow

Icey roads of rain, sleet, and snow
Radio says, stay home if you've no place to go
But the West Main Diner calls saying forget it!
It's only snow, the coffee's on with pancakes cooking slow
Then, what to my wondering eyes should appear?
Dave Clark and his snow moving tribe in their best gear

Hot chocolate and coffee from pots set aside,
Debbie knew they were coming, it's not a surprise
Don "Juan" Kennedy set the tables
Knife, fork, and spoons
With which you could not move much snow
So Dave announces,
Hey guys leave the utensils when you're ready to go!

Hey look! It's all turned to snow
So soon back we will go,
Clearing again everyone that we know
We're the Dave Clark crew,
The tribe with the shovels that worships the snow
Lori singing
Let it snow, let it snow, let it snow
Oh yes! We'll take a coffee to go
Sticky bun anyone?
Wow! Would you look at that snow!

# Oh No! It's Peggy-Sue

Moshe' Mashugana! That's me through and through,
Don't know what I'm doing, but I'll tell you what to do
Now! I went to buy a pickle, good thing I got two
Grabbed a half pound of pastrami, a loaf of rye bread too
And oh! Lordy, lordy here come two-ton Peggy-Sue

Well we all know she is not so kosher,
But said she'd take care of my pickle, did that mean,
Thank god I got two?
Next thing I know,
I've got pickle juice running all over my shoes
Give Peggy-Sue a napkin, three or four will do,
Used up mine, wiping off my shoes
All the time hiding my pastrami and rye
From two-ton Peggy Sue

Always loved Cohen's delicatessen
Corn beef, kosher hot dogs, Matzah balls et al,
But then again there's that woman Peggy-Sue
She's got an eye on what you ordered
So, I say to Melvin, Cohen hold that door,
I'm coming through at least two steps ahead,
Of that two-ton pickle eating woman
Throw her a Matzah ball or two
Slow her down, I'm coming through
Going to enjoy my last pickle if it's the last thing that I do
And not with Peggy-Sue!

# My Birthday Walk

Went to the morgue today
They threw me out
Met two vultures
And they began to shout!
Get out of here, don't come near!
Till you look more
Like a two-day old dead deer

Just looking for love, on my birthday
Trying to find a little cheer coming my way
A Guinness or two, I'm more than happy to pay!
But it seems even the undertaker's upset with me
Tells me, I've been hanging around a little too long
Hanging round much too long, he's telling me!
Well, he can't be planting my very own self
Or even be throwing my ashes, in the deep blue sea

So, I told them all, you can go back home
This kid here's still surfing in Guinness's foam
Too many places to see, places to roam
So, don't you be waiting up, I'm on my way to Athae
Toast Mr. O'Conner, drain some foam
At old Brown Joes, how many pints will we drain,
Until it's time we're dancing all the way home
Buster, Patches, Brown Joe and me
On a birthday walk to see what we'll see
Dancing and surfing on Guinness's foam
Ah! One more pint, then we'll dance our way home

# Angels Don't Wear Camouflage

I never saw an angel wearing camouflage
Good people need neither hood not mask
They simply stand up proud and perform their task
We have no need for King or Queen,
Unless it's the harvest fest
And who needs to live with the taste of vinegar
Emblems of hate upon their vest?
Living with the mob mentality,
Can this be someone's lifetime quest?

Hate, the worst of four-letter words
A word people hide behind with its ugly thoughts and deeds
And when exposed to the light of day you'll soon find,
It can never fulfill anyone's true needs
So, go read a good book about living and forgiving
Change your horizons perhaps educate
Find an angel with a shining face
No hoods, no mask
Nowhere the shadow of that thing called hate

Remember angels need no camouflage
Go find sunshine in the rain
Can't imagine on a death bed tasting the vinegar of hate,
So open your eyes,
It's way, way passed time to shed that weight
And anyone can tell you how good love feels,
So why hesitate?
Unload the burden, live your life
Your heart was meant for love, there is no place for hate
And today's the perfect date!

# Drug Dealing Mama

You're my drug dealing Mama
Pushing my affliction into addiction
And baby, that's as good as it gets
You and your dealing in love and happiness

You're my drug dealing Mama
You and your drug of love
In the back seat, on the couch
Or under the stars above

I'm all about you baby,
You and your drug of love
Concerning my heart as only you can do
Tell ya if I had any, all my money'd be for you

My pusher, my dealer, sure I'd go to jail with you
And I can see it now, the jail house rock
That's what else we'd do
Baby you know because I'm so addicted to you
So, so addicted to you
You're the drug of love baby and I'm so addicted to you
Addicted to you
Drug me mama with love
Love'n me and you

# Tried Their Best

Seems like my gang of friends went out of their way,
To prove the axion
"If you can't do the time, don't do the crime"
Sometimes it was like they were bragging
Hey, look at me I'm doing time!
And when you look at it, they really were not very good,
Pretty poor in fact, at doing crime
They had a knack for getting caught, maybe not in the act
But in a week or so, yeah! Sometimes in the act!
I remember them cleaning out a mansion,
While the occupants were on vacation
With a moving van they stole
Crazily, they got a local policeman to stop traffic,
While they backed the truck onto the property

Of course, they immediately hocked their treasure
Giving the pawn shop their home address, never a good idea
Once they got caught parking illegally
While emptying out a men's clothing shop
The cop said he was going to give them a ticket
Which upset them, so now they decided to show this cop,
Just how dumb he was, Oh yeah! You're so smart?
Well here we are robbing the store,
And you're worried about writing a ticket?
Yes, indeed that did not go over really well,
I've always said there is no percentage
In insulting the arresting officer

Now! Growing up in my neighborhood,
Left plenty of time to play pinochle, sitting on the steps on the corner
so, now I have to believe playing cards in prison,
was like playing on the corner
and passing the time like this worked just fine
because after all there were lots of friends with which to dine
Now I can't imagine being in jail, the army was bad enough!
Yet when I mentioned this, I got the pat answer,

Prisons not so bad!
Well, now no time for me, you kidding me?
I can't stay in the house sometimes
And I never found pinochles being a way of life,
Or pitching pennies very profitable for me

But here's an aside, I run into my buddy Johnny
Walking down the street, fresh out of Gratersford Prison
Needless to say, I was very glad to see him
And now Johnny tells me this story

First you need to know I was running in college at the time
And indoor track was popular on TV, Sunday afternoons
I was running well at the time, and was on some of these shows
Now Johnny proceeds to tell me,
Jimmy, we watched you on television, I told everyone
That's my man! No one can catch him
(luckily, I won some of those races!)
But how crazy is that Gratersford Prison cheering for me,
Like I was one of theirs, never know do we?
I must admit this was very special to me,
Remember no way could I do the time!
And if for a moment I brought some fun to these guys.
That was a blessing for me now I do need to admit.
I did get my early training running from the local cops
Fourteenth district down the streets and alleys of Germantown
Never got caught, never!

I look at myself as very lucky,
only a couple of us went into college, three to be exact
and quite a few did time
there are too many stories of how my friends
earned their way to the big house
it was always an adventure
growing up in the "Cowtown" neighborhood
We did have a couple real good athletes in soccer, baseball, and track
Many great memories back in the 50's and early 60's
It's sad to say some of these colorful friends are now gone
But as they say, the memories linger on

# Doctor; Anesthesiologist of Love

Never felt lonely, until I think of you
The beautiful anesthesiologist who stepped out of the blue
Knocking me out
Without a single drop of your sleeping potion
Just a smile and there I was
Full of loves soothing, yet exciting lotion

Soft as a mist you spoke your name
And my heart knew life would never, ever be the same
Then you asked, was my heart sound?
I said just fine, until you came around
And of course, you knew my words were true
I was under your spell, and everyone knew

Found myself under your spell in that misty quiet
But my heart must have been
Somewhere close to riot
In my fantasy love had arrived
Or were you part of the mist, figment of my dreams
Inducing sleep not reality into this lovers' schemes

And now I've only memories of the doctor of my dreams
She knocked me out, her smile her potion
Just one look brought feelings, as deep as any ocean
To me, she's the girl, the Doctor
The object of all my devotion
More than a dream, more than a dream
One more smile, Doctor, my Queen
I think another operation gonna be one of my schemes

# Don't Ever Give the Queen a Frown

No! No! It's never about the crab cakes
Baby, what's going on inside?
Sometimes, something's surprisingly get us down
And the beautiful Queen, she wears a different crown
But she's too special, she'll never stay down

That's why god made mirrors
So, my Queen, go stand and stare
Drink in the loveliness, the mouth I'd love to kiss
Enjoy that face, a face to fall in love with
Surrounded by a halo of beautiful red hair

Look in that mirror
See what I've seen
And you'll understand why I stare
And know why there's warmth I feel
Whenever you pass, whenever you're near

And so always know, when crab cakes turn brown
And you need some room to breathe
This someone will always be around
To kiss your neck, chase a frown
And of course, he finds it sad and lonely
Whenever you leave town
So anytime my Queen,
Let our kisses change the way we breathe
Let wild, hot kisses change to way we breathe
And tell me I should never leave
Come on Pattie!

# King of the Easy-Pickup

I have to say hello, tell her how beautiful she is
Even among all these lovely faces
The hours passing so fast
Better use all my social graces

Here I am alone and lonely
Yet I know I shouldn't say
That you look so familiar
From somewhere, some other day

Is it my imagination or do I wish it that way?
I'm so bad at names, always remember faces
Oh! You say you're the mother of my children
Yes! I remember, the embraces

May I buy you a drink?
A hors d'oeuvre or two?
Possibly get a ride with you?
You know, I can be a great lover, especially with you!

Wow, it's my lucky night
All my pick-up lines, all my moves worked just fine!
While having so much fun,
Acting like a jerk

Am I cool or what!
Okay, never mind!

# Going to be a Prophet (Make some too)

I'm thinking there's a profit
In my becoming a great prophet, P-R-O-P-H-E-T
So, everyone please, my new address is,
Your Holiness, when you refer to me

Or perhaps, you're Imperial, Emeritus Majesty
Sort of like a young Mohammed Clay Ali
Can you see the person I could be?
Another Joe Prophet, you can call your majesty

So already, here I am your majesty
Time to send a few dollars, pesos, euros
Soon as can be, address it to his imperial majesty
Or maybe, "your Holiness" yeah, that works for me!

Going to get me some long robes
Catch on to that money load
Tell you of things, you'll never see
Or is it the weather person I should be?

Telling you of fifteen-foot snows, you'll never see
No! No! Prophet! P-R-O-P-H-E-T
That's where the big money's sure to be
And I kind 'a really like being called "Your Majesty"
Yes! I'm sure, I could live with "Majesty"

# Beach Cream (it's my new song)

Everybody's at the pool
Singing my new song
'bout smearing on the beach cream
Dancing all day long

Crank up my guitar
Speakers start to scream
Everybody getting wild
'bout the wonders of beach cream

Beach cream, beach cream, rub it on your arms
On your neck and ears, couldn't do no harm
Smear it on your legs and feet
On your nose, but not on the food you eat!

Beach cream, beach cream
SPF-40 to a million, give me sunscreen
Rub some on my back!
Save me, save me baby, from a nasty sun attack

Beach cream, beach cream
Kids hanging 'round the pool
Do the stroll 'n do the slop, rock the teenage scene
I'm picking out the cord's 'n slopping on the cream

We'll play all night and day
A tube of beach cream for our pay
So, girl I'll play my song for you
Just bring along that tube of goo
Beach cream, beach cream
Rub some on me, I'll rub some on you

But don't forget the goo!
Beach creams for me and you!


You do know that now they even have a spray
But baby, we prefer the goo!
Don't you see, beach cream! Beach cream!
That's the only way,
Only the best for you and me

Beach cream come on sing along with me!
Ah, a little Aqua Velva couldn't hurt!

# It's a Birthday Party, Isn't It?

Scarlett, Scarlett, Birthday girl
Scarlett, Scarlett, head full of curls
Blow out all the candles
Make a birthday wish
But, be careful with your ice-cream
Or the dog will clean the dish
Then again, who really cares?
It's a birthday party isn't it?

Big bowls of pretzels, pretzels and chips
Maybe Doritos and some cheesy dip
We'll get mommy to make milkshake delights
Then we'll have to start
Our giant marshmallow fight
Milkshakes and marshmallows
She's gonna have a fit
As everyone shouts! It's a birthday party isn't it?

Happy, happy birthday
Scarlett, dancing, birthday girl
Happy, happy
The best one in the world
Then we'll tell mommy
There's something we have learned
Never put beer in the coffee urn
Oh! Better shout! It's a birthday party isn't it?

It's Scarlett's birthday
P-A-R-T-Y
Isn't it?

# Freddy and his Bacon

It's early morning, before first light
Coffee's the habit
Fried eggs and bacon
And I'm soon out of the hobbit
Watching the sun break the night
And as usual there's Freddy
Going back to his den from an adventurous night
How about, "Crazy the raccoon"
Trying to start a big fight?
Enjoying giving, the neighborhood cats quite a fright

Though the trees are still bare
There's spring in the air
And Mr. Fox, Freddy knows
There's bacon by the bush under the tree over there
I always watch until the bacon and Freddy disappear
Deer in the meadow, birds singing their songs
Bacon in his belly, Freddy's snoring along
And it pays to sit quietly, as the new day begins
As I tell Freddy see you tomorrow
There will be beef under the tree
Sleep through the day, you know you can count on me
Nice piece of beef will be under the tree
We're becoming like buddy's
My man Freddy the fox and me

# Officer Slavin, There's Been a Crime

Hurry Holmes and Watson
Detective Jimmy Slavin
I'm the victim of a crime
We were laughing, smiling, talking
Maybe having too good a time

I had only just learned her name
And then she was gone
She stole away, along with my heart
Life hasn't been the same, when all I have left
Is the memory of her eyes, the wind whispering her name

Isn't this a robbery of sorts?
Can a stolen heart be recovered in court?
Hurry guys and find her
Tell her it's time to surrender to a sentence
Of healing my heart
With more laughing, talking, no more being apart

Tell her hurry back
And forever, forever and ever
She'll have a lock on my heart
Lock us up when you find her

Because I've got a dollar seventy-three
For you if you'll throw away the key

# Please, Pardon Me!

Ever since you said, "we've met!"
My life's one of confusion
As I was at the point of thinking
Maybe you were only an illusion

To me, the cosmos can lose all track of time
Or the sun and moon forget to shine
But to think I may have held your hand in mine
What do they say, "totally, blows my mind?"

Was there a string of pearls adorning you?
How could I have missed so many clues?
Was it witchcraft made my defenses fall
Or the dream, that you were my one 'n all

Possibly I found you,
Miss fascinating, captivating
Too, too precious, more than my dreams could do
Just so, so delicious, wonderful you
Now I'm telling myself, damn! No excuse will do

But! If you're reading this
I'm with the dream that's wonderful you
Asking the gods, what else they can do
While here I am, with wonderful you
Love so, lovely all of wonderful you

# Unlawful Assembly

I think it's called
An unlawful assembly
But I sure appreciate
The way we congregate
And the way we make
A crowd of two
In the perfect rendezvous
Of me and you

Now, how about if we meet
In the middle of the street
Form our own little clique
So, we can shout above the crowd
"I love you too"
How about an
Unlawful assembly, my dearest,
Dear with you?

Or we could always march on City Hall
Tell the judge, don't try to stall
We have money for
The license if needed
Then we'll form our crowd of two
Mr. and Misses, "I'm in love with you"
In a perfect rendezvous of me and you

A perfectly lawful assembly for you and me
The perfect crowd of two just as it should be

# Electronic Zoo (call me, baby)

Facebook, texting, E-mail, Tweeter, it's an electronic zoo
Please don't "friend" me baby, I want to talk to you

Don't want a message, I want to hear your sweet voice
Hear you laugh at my bad jokes, sigh at my sweet nothings
Hear you tell me, I'm your choice

Want to be so personal, baby you're my love,
You're not an app
Don't want to think of you twiddling with a computer
Sitting in your lap

Don't tell me it's convenient to send a line or two
You're much, much too important, I want to talk to you
Want to talk to you baby, if only on the phone
Texting just shows me, that we're both so all alone

So, call me, call me baby if only for a moment or two
So that I can hear how your sweet voice says those things
That makes me want to be with you

Call me, call me baby, love to talk with you
And if you text at all, just say ILU!

Call me, call me baby
Want a talk to you
Want a talk to you

# Dirty Rotten Thieves

Look out people
Here comes the scam
They're rippin off the dudes and dudess
Fast as they can

I'm telling you right now
They'll even steal your teeth
Don't let them see your wallet
They are the lowest, dirty thieves

Telling you they will paint your house
Fix-up your driveway
Don't give them any money
That will only make them go away

They love to sell annuities
If they can get your cash
They'll collect the interest, you might as well
Just leave the money on the couch

Wait until you hear
You won the lottery
Just send a check to cover taxes
You're going to be as rich as you can be

You can smell the rip-off coming
Going to sell you a car
This time the thief's in Africa, in Madagascar
And it doesn't really matter, they never owned the car

Hold tight to your wallet
They are looking for you dude
We're selling you a charity
Send us your money and we'll chose

They're collecting for hurricanes
Or some catastrophes
Just send some money
We're only here to please

They are the nicest people, this low life scum
They will smile right in your face
If you only knew their history
Their morals are a total, total disgrace

So, watch out all you people
Here they come, the dirty, rotten, low life scum
Tell your neighbor, tell your mom
If it sounds too good, you are looking at harm

Don't trust them at all
They're practicing how to use the devil and his charm
They are the very devil,
Hold them back with both your arms
And watch out for those credit cards,
Talking about harm!
They call those devils bankers
And man can they do harm

# Short Stack of Pancakes

Short stack of pancakes
A piece of bacon or two, baby when you're this close
I can't remember, what was on the menu
Guess I'm passed falling, already gave my heart to you
Baby, getting crazy, I'm all about you

Fried eggs 'n bacon
Or is there something else that we can do?
Because in my imaginings,
So many things in my dreams are coming true
Too, too much or just, so in love with you

Ham and French toast
Lost in the warmth of your smile
Couldn't care less if my order, takes a while
I'd have to plead guilty if they put me on trial
Guilty of loving! Guilty of loving such a wonderful smile

Breakfast, well that's an excuse,
You are the reason I'm here with a heart beating like a drum
Hoping a new love past begun
Beef stew will do just fine, if you'll put your hand in mind
Forget the menu, I'm here to see you

Did I say, how I'm so in love with you
Sooo in love a with you
Beef stew?

# Daddy and the Rainbow

Whoever could have known?
That on New Year's Eve to heaven
Daddy had to go?
Or that sunny day at the cemetery
He'd say that he was okay
With a beautiful rainbow
And how is it a six-year-old
Knew Daddy was saying hello, in his own way

How do you explain that forever
We won't see him again
No one can explain with talking
Or the writing of the pen
Or how do we explain that rainbow
That followed all those miles home
Was he saying Scarlett and Chris I love you
I'm so sorry I had to go

Leaving the cemetery mommy said
Daddy will be here if you need to talk or
Just to say hello
From now on this will be your very own
Private place to go
Where Mom-Mom and Daddy in their rest
Will listen because they love you so
And we'll always know they are smiling
Sending love with every new rainbow

Do you know, they say you have his eyes
His love of life
His old golf clubs
But how could anyone know?
That Daddy would be a shooting star,
A beautiful rainbow?

So, Scarlett when you see that spectrum in the sky
Call out!
So, all can know, there he is,
My Daddy, in his beautiful rainbow
And when I go to sleep at night
I'll always, always know
That Daddy loves me so
Forever and forever
My Daddy loves me so!

# Thank You, Thank You, Merci Beaucoup

Thank you, mademoiselle,
Madam, lady, the goddess that's you
Thank you, thank you, merci beaucoup
I never expected to find the beauty of you
Your smile like the lights of the heavens shining through

Merci, merci to the gods above
I asked for a friend and they sent someone to love,
Not just someone but the most beautiful angel
They had up above

So, thank you, thank you, merci beaucoup!
Baby, even if we couldn't speak the language
You can see it in my eyes
And if they could see you now, no one would be surprised

Danke schoen, you silly gods
Merci, merci beaucoup
You sent me a goddess to love
And forever and ever I will follow through

And every time I kiss you, speak your name
I'll always whisper merci beaucoup
My prayer to thank the gods
For the gift that is you
Thank you, thank you
Merci beaucoup

# My Mind Belongs to You

Trying to do my best in a song, try to explain
That my medial prefrontal cortex is a glitch
A reward better than ice cream or cocaine
So, I wrote this song, and it's all true
It's about how my thoughts return to you

Our minds are made to wander
So how could it be true?
That this mind of mine keeps returning, returning dear to you
Now, my psychologist said, that's okay!
Cause that's what love will do
So now at least, I have a clue
As my mind, returns to you

So, they found me in the default mode network
Posterior cingulated,
Medial prefrontal cortexes in a tonic activity
If only, you'd feel it too
They found my emotions and precuneus in a vortex
As minds in love will do
My cortex's in a vortex
I'm so in love with you

I'm told my mind was made to wander
That's what it was meant to do
So why let it relax? I like it like that
Let it just keep coming back,
Coming back, coming back to you
Love what this brain can do

Thinking there is only you

Yes, I've been observing and deducting
But, can't change my point of view
My brain won't relax, as the psychologist said
Heart and mind, I do belong to you
So this, my brain remains, in the old psychology refrain
Totally, really, truly, really nuts for you

Sorry Holmes,
Watson rules!
When only love will do

I really enjoyed your book
Had to read it twice, so I could understand it
Hope this gave you at least a smile
A laugh would be better

# He Stole my Lovely Wife

Gonna sing me a hillbilly country song
So, they can play it on the radio all day long
I'm gonna tell you how she cheated, stole my dog
Left me with the children and one fat hog

She left with my best friend,
But I don't think they got too far
Not driving in my old 1970 Chevy car,
But there they go the two of them
My lovely wife and my best friend

So, you think I'd be down hearted, really blue?
Well, I find myself grinning ear to ear, wouldn't you?
Just wait until things start going south
And she starts a playing the spoons
Singing those beer drinking blues

Now, Jed and I will never need to make amends
We'll always be the best of friends
He'll soon find out, with the beer drinking blues
There is no end, poor old Jed!
With the beer drinking blues, there is no end

Now it's the kids and I and one fat pig
I've gotten out the fiddle, I'm playing a Blue Ridge jig
In a peace and quiet, don't think, we never ever knew
Now that we ain't a listening to the beer drinking blues

Poor o'l Jed!

# Jazz for the Heart

Feels lonely tonight,
Is that a trumpet crying a sad heart song?
What's that song he plays?
What's he trying to say?
Feels like he's taking delight
Adding to this long lonely night

Could he be so mean getting so low down
Setting the scene, killing my dreams
Another night all alone
No one even on my telephone?
Bass man seems to play in such a slow lazy way
Is he another one all alone?
As if from down deep in my soul a low down
Hurting, wailing saxophone
Sure, seems to me everyone's all alone

North Philly's a stop on the train
For Dauphin Street and Coltrane
We can ride to New York, make a few dollars
Buy some non-kosher pork!
For barbeque and some N'Orleans style stew
Saxophone won't you try, fill a few cords with some blues
Should 'a gone to Zanzibar Blue
where Sandoli will play for you
Avant Garde jazz for those in the know, for the few
No more, no more lonely's tonight
Play that music until daylight
Something special and jazzy for the heart
Bass, saxophone, piano do your part
Bring us some of that jazz
The sunshine of the heart

# Turn Up Tara!

Turn up! Turn up!
What's that you sippen'
In your cup?
Turn up, baby
Tripping that libation
Looking so good too,
Gonna have to know your name
Share a drink with you

Turn up, turn up Tara
Partee, 'til the night is through
What yo drinking in that cup?
Cause I'm a guy, never heard turn up
Until I danced with you
And I think they'll find me
When the sun comes up
Sleeping out, drying out, with the morning dew

Now I know when I've been turned up
Yet, I keep thinking, girl of you
Turned up Tara, buttercup
Partee till we're through
Long as I can turn up
Baby doll, with you
So, what's that you sipping in that cup
Loves potion number 2?
(hate rap!)
Cause I'm so in love with you

# Cherry Blossom, Cherry Bomb

You've always got me thinking of cookies and cream,
Of how precious you, stepped out of a dream
Lips cherry blossom pink, eyes big as the sky
Cherry bomb kisses, you are the 4<sup>th</sup> of July

Peaches and cream, beauty evergreen
You, my divine lady, you've always been the dream
And unlike the tracings of the moon,
So easy can I lose my way
One look at you and stars are shining,
In the middle of the day

A cherry bomb kiss, and the fire has begun
Oh, for the warmth of our room a place
Where the stars can meet the sun
Cherry blossoms, cherry bombs
Hearts overflowing to exploding
If only in a dream, forever has begun

You are the softest pink, the serenity of a blossom in the sun,
You set my heart to beating like a heavy metal drum?
So "hot pink" let the moon lose its way
The stars rule the day
Take my hand, burn my lips, let me believe in the promise
That for now, you'll be here to stay

Cherry blossom, cherry bomb, the image of your beauty
In this heart will last forever, ever and a day
The 4th of July, oh yes! I'll always think of you that way
Always! Tracie,
Always think of you this way

# Going to See Sarah Run

So, I'm flat broke
Flat, flat broke
So just pie and coffee for me,
Broke enough to even try a cup of tea
But give it a day, money's coming in
And then it will be filet mignon, a very good wine for me

I'll bet that no one remembers that I was of the manor born
Riding around in a Cadillac, Rolls Royce
And the chauffeur sometimes let me play with the horn
But today who would know I was of the manor born
Now that I'm flat broke
All the money's gone

But, the coffee's great, waitress so fine
Pie good enough that I need not much, to occupy my mind
Need no Cadillac, I've a bell on my bike
Weather's so beautiful, what's not to like?

Now, off to watch the race
Up and down the river drive
I know that Sarah, my friend's going to run great
It's a half marathon?
Man, that would seal my fate
I'll be cheering her on, me, this flat broke bloke
Of course, she doesn't know it,
Not that she'd care

I'd be her biggest fan except her mom is also here
Woah! Here she comes
"Go Sarah!", "looking good", "Way to run!"
You know, I think I'm so much cheering as a fan,
Than if I tried to run
Go! Go! Sarah!
I hope you're having fun!
Princess Hanrahan,
In your running shoes
I hope you're having fun

# Sauce or Gravy?

So, there we were, two tally guys
And me debating one of the great arguments
You can find yourself in on the streets of Philly
Is it sauce or gravy?

Now I'm about to tell you where the truth lies
And of course, I know I'm right!
Let me explain,
Now sauce is red, made of tomatoes
And gravy's brown made for meat and potatoes
Cheese steak sauce and onions
Now for you foreigners, that's anyone outside city limits
What you do is take a crusted roll
twelve to twenty inches long
fry up some chipped steak and some onions
American cheese you lay over the meat
As it finishes, put it in the center of said roll,
Now with a ladle, you dip into the pot of "sauce"
And spread it down the middle of the roll
There it is, a Philly cheesesteak, sauce and onions
Not gravy! Did I say sauce?

Now! How about a Salisbury steak and mashed potatoes?
Now we need some gravy! Remember gravy's brown
Hot roast beef sandwich with gravy
Happens the world around
Suburban peoples can be brought to wonder,
"what the hell are we talking about?"
Yet derision such as this can cause unbelievable damage,
Families break up, "Bocci" teams disbanded,
Friends refusing a glass of wine,

105

Bookies no longer playing sleight of hand,
Drive by shootings


Can even lose its glamour
When ordering your pasta marinara
You've no need to ask for sauce
It's in the name marinara sauce
And I could rest my case, however
Let's get back to the chase


Once again, being diplomatically astute as I am
I'm talking to Joe Battaboots, and one thing Joe knows
Is that sauce is red, gravy's brown
And South Philly knows
That this is what makes our world go around


Cheese steak, sauce and onions, what a beautiful sound
Pass the macaroni
The sauce and meatballs the table around
Try not to laugh at the Bocci team,
Old men, try to get them to laugh and wipe off that frown
As their hernia makes it hard
To pick their balls up off the ground


106

# Vote a Woman for God!

God can't be an old white man
I came to that conclusion today,
No way, no way, no way!
Am I accepting that, no way!
Yep, I came to that conclusion earlier today
Old men become politicians
Spend their day lying and denying for pretty good pay
Raising money so they can stay in a job
Becoming multi-millionaires on a $200,00 salary
Stealing all the way

So, tell me do you really think God's a boy
Playing with us like soldier toys
When he has a whole universe to visit every day?
Well I'm thinking come November
We should vote him out
As a woman would do a better job
Well, remember this
When a man is dying on a battlefield
He calls for mommy, not his god!

So, let's put god on the ballot
We all know too many times,
He has been sleeping on the job
Pestilence as virus has gotten carried away
A guy named Hitler came out to play
Dementia had his finger on the bomb
I'm about to rest my case
God on the ballot, Lizzy Warren,
Amy Klobuchar, Susan Rice?
Let them have their say,

Questioning him on what did you do today?
Does he know Corona's no longer lime and beer
And we're asking people please don't get near?
A woman would have nursed us, rehearsed us
And gave out the news, such as don't run with sticks
You'll put someone's eyes out,
Run with scissors and your gonna die, and stop to think
When was the last time he gave you a clue about the lottery
A fast horse or the number of the day?
Now don't you think you should read my bumper sticker,
"vote for Misses someone, for God today!"

No more grumpy old men for God
Telling you what to think and say
A woman on the ballot in November
Time to send old man "Mr. God" on his way
I know women like to talk but unlike men
They even know how to listen
Something that has been lost on we men since old earth
Was born and christened

Well it's not so long a drive to the diner in the morning,
But it got me to thinking, God what cha been doing?
From the fascist in the White House (yeah! We did that!)
To a pandemic that chicken soup won't cure
I know you have a sense of humor,
But it's not funny anymore
So, I'm proposing a woman for God! You go take a rest,
Too, too many have died in your name,
So, we're voting in November
Time to change the game
So, vote in November for a woman
We really need a change!

# Hold the Fries

No fries baby! Please hold the fries
I've been getting too fat, eating with my eyes
So, if you will, won't you hold the fries

That old racoon is once again out in the dumpster
He has been coming around for years
So, I know he is no youngster
Now, I could try to bring the fries to him
But I'd be eating them on the way
And leftovers would be slim

Everyone knows, fries equal many hours in the gym
But even that is better than that ubiquitous double chin
Oh, won't you hold those fries' baby
Or I'll be bursting from within

Oh yeah! Oh yeah! Blame it on the fries
Not the Whisky or the Gin
Not to mention that Cabernet dribbling down my chin

Won't you hold those fries pretty lady
Don't let me give in
I need to save a few calories
Make room for a Manhattan, tonic and some gin
Tell em pretty Momma
We really don't see no double chin!

# Saint Oxymoron

I got to thinking
We need a new church
That can bring together church and state
A church for atheist known as St. Oxymoron's
I could also volunteer to be a high or low priest
Perhaps an altar boy with no altar
No! no fancy robes
Just be cool, make the scene


No psychopaths allowed or anyone else that's mean
Agnostics are welcome if they'd like to take in the scene
As I don't really know the difference
I guess it's what you do or don't feel like you believe


Now you'll never hear us say, come and bring your money
No way, we'd rather have you walk up and say something
Funny, calling us, brother, sister, cousin or friend
We'll sit around and talk until we either get tired
Or get to the part they call the end

Now, how about those apples?
St. Oxymorons!
The church for atheists, agnostics, Catholics, Hindus
Or anyone else who enjoys talking and being friends
Joking, laughing, having fun until the rising of the sun
Or we call it to an end

Our motto will be
"Come to St. Oxy's,
Bring your old jokes, meet new friends"
Pianos, guitars, congas, bongos, harmonicas, trumpets
whatever
Peace to your belief my friend!

# Wayne's Hot Chili

Got me a bowl of Wayne's four alarm chili on this rainy day
I got here before the lunch bunch,
In time to hear the cook say
We've got chili on the menu today!
He said it out loud
And I said Debbie, how about I order some,
Good thing I got here before the crowd

Spicy, hot chili with tabasco even if it is too much for me
Sometimes I even wear a frown
As I partake and shovel it down
Mercy, mercy, how good can it be?
Rainy day, chili, Debbie and me
Rainy day, what can I say
Kaiser roll, big bowl of chili
Debbie that cute little waitress, what's left to see?

Look at those kidney beans floating in the seams,
Reminding me of trying to run through the rain
Through and in between
Just think! Five alarm fire, Debbie stirring my desires
Me saying, Debbie! Debbie!
How's about another bowl for me?

Yes! Another bowl of chili for me!
Five alarm must be the charm
Red-hot chili for me

Debbie's smile and Wayne's red-hot, tasty chili for me

# New Car

A new car's what I'm looking for
I have no idea, two or four door, just not sure
Red, black or blue, white's looking pretty good too
Yeah, a car shiny new, no candy wrappers, new carpets
A roof that let's in the sun and the rain, should I do?
I think I'm looking for comfort over the long miles
Then there's that lady telling you to go right or left
And stay in your lane,
As she guides you the long way around
Style and comfort, is it important about miles per gallon?

Tell that salesman I'm just looking!
And I'll let him know
If I find something I think's real cooking
A new car, sedan, SUV
One thing I know is no pick-up for me
Perhaps a Rolls Royce
Or would a Porsche be a better choice?
Always loved spoke wheels all shining in chrome
That new car smell although it doesn't last very long
Or very well

Wow! Would you look at that! a car parking itself
Man, I could put my driving skills on the shelf
Now they are pushing four-wheel drive
And we haven't even seen a flake of snow
Vinyl upholstery maybe leather trim
Nothing sweet as a brand-new clean driving machine

Consumer reports has been a big help in my search
Helping me move things right along
Don't want to be rolling the dice or chasing recalls
Soon as that car becomes mine
What do you think, isn't that silver gray one looking fine?

# Cheap Operator

This is the story of a son in law that owes me a beer,
A couple of them
He has his Capo, Steve deliver a five-dollar bill
Trying to but me off!

I cannot believe what a cheap damn back-hoe operator he is!
Five dollars, you kidding me?
It should have been twenty dollars plus interest,
Over all these years
Adding up to a mortgage
A happy hour drink at Casey's
Why not just throw me under an eighteen-wheeler?
If nothing else "Steve" could have worn a suit and tie
I'm telling you I get no respect!

Anyway!
It is good to know that guilt finally caught up to him
And at least he sent me a lousy five dollars
Now, being the most gracious person that I am,
Do not worry, I won't tell a soul,
Just anyone that buys my book

By the way I was sending this particular 5'er back to you
Because I've been led to believe it's counterfeit
And you were just trying to get me in trouble
And I also don't know if I can trust Steve either
Diabolical, the two of you?
I can see the headlines now!
Man tries to pass fake five, at local establishment

So, I sold that fiver to a bandit for pennies on the dollar
I found me five ones from a street person who knew Johnny
And the first thing he said was,
Man, you are smart not trusting that boy and Steve
From H&K
Send that money back
And tell him he'd better get his ass down to Casey's
And buy at least two rounds
Ain't no time to play, and once again he said,
Watch out for those two guys from H&K
Called me, "my man" and to live to drink another day!

Signed, by me,
"one of the really best people you know!"

# Don't You Just Hate It

Don't you just hate it when he makes things rhyme?
Seems he's doing it all the time
Drives me crazy like he doesn't care
Then he'll talk so nice about sunlight in your hair

He'll ask me Tara, doing well in school?
I hope you do lots of reading, it's an important tool

Told my cousin Tyler he was doing fine
Playing his guitar, playing it in time
Tyler said don't you just hate it,
When he makes things rhyme?
I said oh Tyler he does it all the time
Told me he doesn't, it's all in my mind

So, I told him I'm studying the Civil War
Would he rhyme that?
He said probably not, without his General's hat!
Kelly said now that I'm a cheerleader I can jump real high!
He said I know,
When I got here, I saw you falling from the sky

We asked Buster the dog how does he survive?
He said he works out for hours at the local gym,
And when he gets home, he pays very little attention to him!
We looked at each other and said in perfect time,
Don't you hate it when he makes things rhyme!

Pop-Pop said, Tyler get your guitar
We're going to sing a song about my car
Rock'n and rolling in 4/4 time
Anything else would be a crime


Then he started singing gonna drive my school bus
Right through the traffic that they call rush!
Down the highways and the byways
Until we cause a traffic jam
And you know I'll never get those kids to hush


So, we told him a new rule,
There will be no more rhyming here in school
Then we looked at each other,
Said is this a new virus we've discovered? Oh no!
We must have caught the rhyming flu
Cause Pop-Pop here we are rhyming, just like you
Then all the kids in school said,
Didn't they just break the rule?
About rhyming here in school
And we heard everyone say,
"Don't you just hate it when they make things rhyme?"
Man! Oh man! Everybody's doing it, all of the time!

# Old? Nah! I Just Remember

Thinking back to my days of knights
In their flowing robes of bright color
Boldly slipping through the shadows of night,
To find "me lady" in her chambers
All a dazzle in candlelight
A place in the palace where he has come to honor her wishes
And leave before the rising sun or the new day has begun
We knew to leave long before her handmaids
Bring to her a breakfast of prepared tasty dishes

Mid-day and the joust have now begun
It is a place where said knight will dedicate his feats of skill
After accepting her favor on bended knee
It is the unspoken promise to satisfy her needs
Then after a bathing and brush
Sir knight will no longer carry the slight aroma of his steed

But as the years go by, I must admit,
That, these days, the back seat of a Chevy surly beats
Lances, swords, and the aroma of horse droppings
Aqua Velva replaces those traces and a soap called Caress
Leaves you smelling your best

No more need for shining armor,
But her colors I will wear
And just enjoy whatever color she makes of her hair
So! You think I am getting old?
Well! One squirt of Aqua Velva and watch me do bold!

# Can You See Me Being Rich?

If I were a rich man, well there I go again!
Maybe I should play the lottery,
Where there are odds of a billion numbers verses me

If I were a rich man, what fun, how neat would that be?
I would be driving down through town,
Window down, throwing money all around
Yeah! Me in the car throwing money near and far
To people on the street or wherever they are
I'd set the family up with as many silver cups,
They might even find something to like about me

If I were a rich man, I would need a real nice new car,
Maybe a chauffeur to drive me to the bar
Or maybe near and far
How about a sports model, the faster I could go
Let the money flow
After all you can't take that money with you when you go
Let me put the top down, go laughing like a clown
Spread happiness around

Old as I am, there was a time I made good money
And I'm proud to say I've spent it all, along the way
I enjoyed the seasons, especially the fall, my favorite of all
And all I can say, is if I were a rich man,
The greatest feeling would be giving it away
Give someone a real good day

# Memories are like Déjà Vu

We call it the dead of winter
Yet here I stand in the new falling snow
Just having left the warmth and brightness
Of hearth and home
Ah, the snow, fresh and beautiful
Covering lawn and street on the eve of Christmas day
Excitement, filling hearts and floating on air
Because "Santa" is on his way

It's as if I am living a life of déjà vu
Yes! I've been here before
I have seen the lights in the windows,
Decorations on the lawns
New snow making it look as if a new world has been born
I can easily get lost in memories of Christmas long, long ago
Like that kid jumping over or into that three-foot drift
Sledding on the hill, sliding down the street
I am looking at the circle of life
Déjà vu proving that history does repeat

A man stands by the corner waiting for the bus,
Folks hurrying home with bags of presents
Almost at journeys end
Calling "Merry Christmas!"
to strangers and to the best of friends
From the house I hear Nat King Cole on the radio
Competing with Bing Crosby on the TV
Everyone thinking they are singing just for me!
And here I am searching the sky,
Now if only a sleigh I could see

Then there were the days of the mid-night mass
As we dressed in suit and tie
What pretty girls we'd see
And when mass was done, then started the fun
Hitting that one special girl with a snowball,
And running away after all, she might talk to me!
Then off to the all-night diner
Coffee and Lemon Meringue pie
Got to admit she is the apple of my eye
Wonder if she would really talk to me?

Déjà vu is such a great way to say
As we listen to our children
Singing our favorite Christmas songs,
Telling the same stories, eating the same treats
Running and sliding down the middle of the street
The cycle of life renewed, but not in your Christmas shoes!

Time to over dress them and go and see the holiday lights
In the windows and along the avenue
As in my mind I send a missive with a tear and a sigh
Thinking of family and friends
Their smile and the laughter in their eyes
Déjà vu is such a wonderful thing
Especially when out of nowhere it comes as a surprise

Now! Look at me looking, still looking
Searching the sky
A reindeer, a sleigh, can you just imagine if I saw
The miracle of the Santa guy?

# Rummaging's

Days move so fast, seasons pass
Yet memories, special thoughts, come and go
Sometimes like a lightening flash
I had a wife, a lover who shared good and bad
That died too soon, too young
Another example to all mankind revealing that
As men we have no control, we are hopelessly weak
Just witnesses offering hope and love but having no cure

We live within the frame of ourselves and our experiences,
Therefore, we must be special, on top of our game
This is me what can go wrong? And then it comes
That learning the hard way, life giving and taking away
There never were guarantees you will have another day
No guarantees, no returns, just a hole in your heart
Another awful lesson learned
If you are lucky life will move on,
You will find more hopes and dreams
You can spend years in hopes and prayers,
Praying on your knees
Some hearts will bleed, some will succeed, some will say
God saved me for another day
While everyone else succumbed
Someone who in every way was just as special
In every way as you

So, bless yourself as you step up to bat
But please do not think for a minute
That God really cares if the Yankees or Eagles win
And let us not be so naïve as to believe that we call,
"people of the cloth", have any more insight into heaven,
Than the least of us
Be skeptical when they ask you to take the bible as fact

There is so much fiction there
That you can find anything you want
So, do not be surprised when it confuses you!

Think for yourself
Too many charlatans and con artists are there,
Collecting money and remember when they give advice,
That "wise men don't need it and fools won't heed it!"
Let the theologians' study and argue heaven and earth
But remember,
More people have been murdered in the name
Of someone's god and religions,
Than by the greed of all nations

Does God really care? I think not!
Or who can explain to me genocide and holocaust,
How could this occur?
Can a god be this vindictive
Can a god be so callous to pain and suffering?
Can he or she be so disappointed in the image and likeness
That God himself created?

Whoever coined the word "hypocrisy",
Could never imagine how it has become a staple today?
People calling themselves Christians or evangelicals,
That live by lies and never heard of Christian charity
Finding hate for their fellow man
Because of their race, religion, sexual persuasion,
Or the status of being poor
I don't know, I can't explain, just rummaging around!

What could he have been thinking?
This dirty faced kid from Germantown

# Today's Angels Wear Scrubs

How about that?
I am just realizing that today's angels,
Are all dressed up in scrubs
I mean I always knew that these people called nurses,
Always treated us like we were the ones,
That just arrived from above
I watch them scurry from bed to bed
A mask hides their beauty, but not those smiling eyes
And as we hear them speak,
The depts of their warmth and caring,
Of a sudden we realize

Amazing
Their caring hour after hour, day after day,
Chit-chatting with those in need
Like that new puppy bringing joy to the moment
Chasing doubts
Bringing a strength
When the most of us would be getting weak kneed
Nurses! Nurses indeed!

129

They are angels in scrubs letting smiles abound
Even when life around them gets difficult, never a frown
They share a laugh, a retort, the small blessings they find
And you know they will never retreat, there is no time
As once again they are called and go scurrying around!
And I think that if only I were a rich man
Jewels and hosannas, I would lay at their feet
Nurses and their support staff
Each one a little different, each one so neat
And then there's Joanne!
Wow what a treat!

# Civilization's Pandemic Dance

Back in the 50's and 60's
We were always making up new dances
The stroll, the slop, the mashed potato, the twist,
The Bristol stomp and on and on
4:00 and Bandstand was our bible
And you's better be as good a dancer as your rival

Well here we are sixty years later
House bound in the middle of a pandemic
Wondering just what can I do?
I'm starting to think maybe a new dance, who knew?
But I'm finding out that it isn't too easy
This dancing while sitting on the couch
Couches never dance
They sure can be used for romance, but just can't dance
And this dancing in place while sitting still,
Sure, ain't gonna cure anyone's ills

So, I have worked out this one move
I grab the clicker (sometimes called the remote)
Hold it high, push a number
See what appears before your eyes, don't like what you see?
Try it again 1-2-3, jump up, jump up, wash your hands
And when in company be the "Lone Ranger" wear a mask
Do not dare "Shake a Hand!"
Forget what Bill Haley said
Those were different times, so go ahead, use your head!

How is it that we haven't learned
From the very astute Japanese that over all these years
We can show deference to all with a bend of the waist,
The same act replaces a hug or the shaking of hands
It's more than another way of maintaining separation
Or the spreading of germs, it's so much more,
It's a civilized dance, so save the Tango for romance
And then again only with that special someone
There is no reason to be taking a chance
If you think this dance is too much for you
Then have the courage to reach out,
Speak out and simply say,
"I love you!"

So, here I sit, Boogie Woogieing with the couch
Slowly, slowly becoming more than quite a slouch
Seems it is time I figured this out!
So, how is this for a pandemic dance
Take a tip from Mister me, just you wait and see
The maternity wards in December and January!

Now that's civilization's pandemic dance
The one that sure appeals to me!
Yes! My dear we will start with the Tango
Get off the couch
Oh, by the way, did I say
You sure appeal to me?

# Ode To Wolfgang

I went over to Vienna
To find some music, so I said!
However, the Viennese gave me sausages instead
Thought I'd find a little frauline
They gave me oomph-pa-pa
And quite a variety of bread
Music, girls, sausage, site seeing, farm fresh eggs,
But! No lieder hosen to chafe these sensitive, errant legs

Beethoven and Mozart
Found music in the air
Me? I found a landlady
With many pounds to spare
Told me she was my haus frau
With so many sights to see
And she's been saving plenty
Oomph-pa-pa, oomph-pa-pa for me

So, Wolfgang, my friend
I hope you had better luck
Much! Better luck than me
And if you happen to oomph-pa with the landlady
Seasick pills you'd better seek
Please excuse the indelicacies, but! I just had to speak
Better the security in a cathedral, any day of the week!
Just remember, you're going back at night, to sleep?

Oh my!
My oomph-pa-pa
Oh my!
Better you than me

134

# The West Main Breakfast Saga

A not so early morning and the West Main Diner's all a buzz
People holding their cup of coffee, as if it were life itself.
Tell you, for a shot of caffeine, it's like they fell in love
They are some of our favorites, these people, we all know
Some special friends, offering well wishes without end
Now, I'm sure it's true
That we can't do Diner food for breakfast, lunch and dinner
And if you do, I'm telling you
That's not the way to get much thinner
Hey, life is good!
Here we are with all this here talking and complaining
About the sun, the snow or even the raining
Coffee, people, the old neighborhood
Some lady told me mister!
Don't you be eating those potato chips,
Those things are known to hang around
For six months on your hips
Sticky buns to burgers so big
That you can't hold them with one hand
So! Now! Let me tell you about the beautiful waitresses
Oh yeah! Your gonna think life is really, really grand

Then there's Proprietor Wayne, tell how hard he's working
But no respect will he get
As we ask him is it our chain he's jerking?
He'll laugh and threaten to burn our eggs and toast
Or maybe move the West Main to the other coast
Who said, will you fill our cups before you go?
Tell the movie stars we said hello
Scrambled eggs sunny side up,
Maybe just fill the top half of the cup
No respect will he get!


Young Wayne's in the kitchen making fantastic macaroons
But truth be known he'd be much happier home on his couch
Watching Rocky and Bullwinkle cartoons
Oh no! no respect does anyone get, just walk into this room
As Don Juan Kennedy trails the ladies around
As if he was the groom
And I'm thinking that those people
He sailed with on the Mayflower must have been religious
As they never threw him off the boat,
For telling the same old jokes
Especially the ones that made the Pharo croak


But! There again that's the West Main Diner
Fellowship, great food, laughs to change a mood
Waitresses so pretty their touch would fly you to the moon
What! You need a coffee spoon?

# Opiniated Hooliganism

We've been practicing opinionating for quite a few years
We are the over sixty shall we say
Old fan club we love
Telling the same old stories, almost bringing you to tears
Then one of us will say, it was good enough for me
So, it should be good enough today
How did we get so opinionated, does it come with age?
Yet! I'm betting, that giving the chance, none would go back
And spend a day

Oh, how we like to agree with ourselves,
Seems I always gotta be right
Talking of our unique experiences, telling the same old jokes
Why wouldn't the people around us not refer to us
As the old folks?
Yes! We are the opinionated Hooligans
Yes, all the answers we do possess
Now if only we could remember what the hell
We were talking about
While getting our grievances off our chest

Then someone said, hey you old buggers,
Leave the women alone!
Grab a seat at the counter,
Just don't make that seat your home
You hooligan curmudgeon,
keep your opinions to your own self
Your coffee in your cup

# She's No Mirage

Traveling, traveling across the sea
Into the desert where a belly dancer named Jasmine
Is making eyes at me
Showing off her décolletage
Make no mistake, that lady Jasmine, well! She's no mirage

A camel seems to be calling me
From way out on the periphery
A warning of, keep your hands in your pockets
Or chances are could be the last time any part of your money
You're gonna see

Now, you may be the Don Juan of your neighborhood,
But Kennedy! In the Casbah,
That smile ain't going to work so good
Thirty shekels for a five-shekel cup of tea? Buyer beware!
But! Know what! Jasmine, yeah that Jasmine
That jasmine's starting to look kind a real good to me
You know, silk scarf, décolletage, so far across the sea
Waiter, tell me, where's the closest motor lodge?

Silk scarf, the music, almond eyes, looking at me
I'm thinking, it's not so bad, this trip across the sea
Getting to know Jasmine, even met a camel
And he's still calling me

# Apologies Your Majesty

Dear poor Queen your Majesty

You are going to earn your keep today
Yes, it may be argued you've over done your stay
Not mine to say
But rather bring your attention to the moron
You are soon to meet, a selfish child
That, never, ever learned to play
Wait until you catch the act
Of the horses a** we've sent your way
Oh! Britannia what can we say?
But why on god's earth would you permit on your soil
Someone whose only thought in his mind is to despoil?

A person with not one redeeming feature or quality
That when in his presence is so easy to see
He is so, so bad that when he leaves
You'll be questioning your own sanity

So! My dear Queen, Ma'am!
Please accept my apology,
And please know, he would not be there, were it up to me
God Bless You!

Your patience will need all the blessings due

142

# Joel Lambs Friday Place

Another familiar Friday night with the same familiar scene
How many times spent with the music of the night
Bennett and Sinatra's songs for life's background
Laughing with friends, same old friends
Who on Friday nights are always around
The bar is getting crowded, as new arrivals announce
Hey! It's snowing hard and covering the ground

Joel's the man, the bartender, who can merely raise a brow
In the language of, ready for another?
Joel, bartender emeritus the man has been around
He's been there for people with the happies
The forlorn, the bar room clown, the sports enthusiast
He just likes to see you coming around
Okay! One more, one more!
Then I'm off to make the rounds!

Off to see the new snow blanketing the town
A scene so beautiful that it makes for rejoicing
No time for loneliness, wallowing in self-pity
Or wearing a frown
The sounds of traffic, honking here, a silence there
It's like Gershwin's, "Serenade in Blue"
Snowflakes by the thousands dance in the streetlights
As I walk on through
Snowflakes, memories, wonderful thoughts of you
Another familiar Friday night
Visiting our familiar places
Wish I was with you

# Epilogue

So, why did I put this book together when everyone knows, I could have been a biblical scholar, up until the time they threw me out of church. And then again not surprisingly, I could have been a surgeon if I could stand the sight of blood. Even could have climbed Mount Everest but dealing with heights is not quite my idea of an afternoon delight. I thought of running a deli but of course I knew, I'd eat everything in sight.

My buddy Billy Chipin once said, become an agnostic, but you had to see Mom take a fit! So, here I am wondering, what was I thinking? You think I had better get a grip? I was thinking of calling Al Franken, he is a Harvard graduate you know. I heard he had a way to tell, exactly where to go.

There was a time I thought of heading for the Emerald Isle but found out even the Irish were confused. Do you know that not that long ago the mayor of Dublin was a Jew? But I bet he never met my friend Harry from page 39, who if he ran out of fresh fish at his store, he'd still find a way to get a coin from you.

So, this book of nonsense was all that was left for me to do, and for the sum of fifteen dollars a copy, this book I'll lay on you. Or you may be interested in a signed copy for $14.95 plus five cents for the ink. Mea coupe! What do ya think?

# Acknowledgements

**Kelly Simmons:** formatting and set-up

**Tyler Simmons:** computer and mathematics guru

**Sean McCleery:** a true investigator, arranger and conductor

To:

The many friends and mentors who guided me while growing up in the city of Philadelphia, where ethnicity was there for the taking. They proved to me that there were so many great people in every walk-in life, nationality, race and belief. There were those that shared their ways of life and philosophies, their food, music, athletic prowess, wants desires and warmth. All in their own way showing that once young man how to grow into a life well lived and enjoyed.

# Other Works

### *Cherry Blossoms*
A book of love songs and poems

### *Snowflakes*
A book of Christmas songs and poems, some of which have
already been recorded

These help make up the trilogy with *What Could I Have
Been Thinking?*

All are now available at BookBaby, Barnes & Noble,
Amazon, your local bookstore or by sending a check for
$15.00 directly to Jim Flannery

### *Greetings of the Season*
The Christmas CD that has for the last ten years shared
world-wide acclaim can also be purchased. If purchased with
a book direct from Jim only $10.00. It is also available
through CdBaby, iTunes and Spotify